ABANDONED ARIZONA

MINING AND MEMORIES

SUSAN TATTERSON

AMERICA
THROUGH TIME®
ADDING COLOR TO AMERICAN HISTORY

For Hepburn and Bacall—my babies—you make sitting at the computer writing and editing photos so much more enjoyable.

America Through Time is an imprint of Fonthill Media LLC
www.through-time.com
office@through-time.com

Published by Arcadia Publishing by arrangement with Fonthill Media LLC
For all general information, please contact Arcadia Publishing:
Telephone: 843-853-2070
Fax: 843-853-0044
E-mail: sales@arcadiapublishing.com
For customer service and orders:
Toll-Free 1-888-313-2665

www.arcadiapublishing.com

First published 2019

ISBN 978-1-63499-205-3

Typeset in Trade Gothic 10pt on 15pt
Printed and bound in England

CONTENTS

PREFACE

One of the joys of heading off on an adventure to photograph the locations for the Abandoned Union series of books are the road trips. I have lost track of the thousands of miles I have wandered so far! Oftentimes, though, the planned route will take many detours, and before I know it, the book I am intending to photograph turns into another. *Abandoned Arizona: Mining and Memories* kept me close to home—comparatively—but the research for the chapters led me down as many "rabbit holes" as the detours on the road trips.

One of the most exciting research discoveries for this book was learning one of my idols, Dorothea Lange, had photographed the same areas in Casa Grande. Lange was a preeminent and pioneering documentary photographer who traveled the country for the Farm Security Administration, and her Depression-era portraits express the hardship and pain of the times while commanding visual empathy. Her images of immigrant cotton laborers and their camps in the Casa Grande area, although not as well-known as her iconic image "Migrant Mother," which hangs in the Library of Congress, still bear her powerful narrative style.

Local history is often multi-layered and centuries deep and can open doors to our past and our future. Arizona's geologic riches share more than 1,000 years of history with the state's agricultural development. Hundreds of years before the Spanish arrived, Native Americans mined and farmed Arizona's bountiful terrain. Today, modern mining ruins and abandoned farms populate diverse regions of the state and offer the curious explorer much insight into centuries-old mining techniques and farming practices. What remains illuminates the past and chronicles our unceasing lightning-speed submission to newer technologies and our desertion of land now devoid of its spoils.

Abandoned Arizona: Mining and Memories delves, photographically, into several of Arizona's sparsely settled mining and farming areas. Wandering through Southern Pinal County's forgotten farms is reminiscent of a visit to a Smithsonian exhibition of antique agricultural machinery and superseded industrial processing methods. Mines, too, leave their mark, and not just in the land they scar—their crumbling remains are testimony to the grit and determination of the West's early settlers. Many of these once-bustling agricultural and industrial sites will one day be erased and succumb to our voracious hunger for urban sprawl. The images in *Mining and Memories* will remain as testimony to Arizona's proud history as a land of exceptional beauty and natural bounty.

As always, I have many people to thank for the information they helped me gather; it was particularly difficult for this edition as several of the locations have little documented history and many phone calls were made trying to track down former owners or anyone associated with the properties. A very big thank you to Stephanie Joyner, Executive Director of the Pinal County Historical Society Museum; her tireless efforts to uncover information about the 96 Ranch were largely unsuccessful but greatly appreciated. With that said, the wonderful archive of newspaper articles she unearthed on the fabled Florence "Coke Ovens" led me to spend far too many hours immersed in their history and wonderful tall-tales of their origin.

I am grateful to my colleagues at Central Arizona College, Skyla Teel and Marcia Iselin, for "knowing someone, who knew someone;" their help and interest in my work is invaluable. A special thank you to Bridgette Pagel and her father, Frank P. Encinas; without Frank's knowledge of how cotton gins work, I would have been at a loss to describe the machinery I photographed. My crazy, adventurous friend and former colleague Diane Beecroft; I could not have reached the Charcoal Kilns without her UTV (the beast that can tackle any desert terrain), and I have her to thank for helping me reach places that are completely inaccessible to even the toughest Jeep! The generous strangers who returned my calls and emails, Henry Freeman and Joe Foust—thank you!

And last but certainly not least, Heather Moulton, my sidekick; although she only joined me on the trip to Eden for this edition, she was with me in spirit and is, as always, the generous keeper of correcting my grammatical errors.

I am sure there are more acknowledgments due, but I am out of space, and off to my next adventure! I hope these photographs inspire your curiosity as much as the places have mine. Keep adventuring!

Sue Tatterson
Gold Canyon, 2019

CLIFTON

Clifton stands resolutely only a few miles east of Morenci and Morenci Mine; an encroaching behemoth, the mine has swallowed two historic mining towns in its lust for the largest copper reserves in the United States. Clifton was founded in 1873 and was part of the Clifton-Morenci District or, as it was otherwise known, the Copper Mountain District. The towns of Old Morenci and neighboring Metcalf were demolished and enveloped, more than fifty years ago, by the largest open-pit mine in Arizona. Today, Clifton, stoic in its survival, proudly promotes the importance of its history as not only a mining town but as an integral part of the fight for mining workers' rights.

Historic Chase Creek Street (Copper Avenue), once the town's central business district, where in 1915–16 hundreds of striking workers marched peacefully, is lined by architecturally significant buildings standing in varying stages of disrepair and decay. In some cases, only the facade remains, as is the case with the former Lyric Theatre; built by Joaquin Estavez, it was modeled after the Alhambra in Spain. Most of the buildings that remain today were built in 1913, after a devastating fire tore through and destroyed twenty-five structures.

Clifton has survived not only fire and man's ravenous need for copper, but its location on the San Francisco River has seen it withstand thunderous floodwaters. On October 1, 1983, the normally peacefully flowing river became a force to be reckoned with. It crashed its way through the town at a frightening pace of 90,000 cubic feet per second. Once again, Clifton rebuilt, and today what remains intact among the decaying and abandoned structures stands as testimony to the tenacity of the small town's residents and a passionate historical society.

Remains of the Clifton smelter, which operated in the late 1800s–early 1900s.

Clifton smelter foundations.

Wall after wall of bricks are almost all that remains of the smelter.

Abandoned tanks at the base of the smelter.

An abandoned Texaco maintenance shed adjacent to the smelter ruins.

Smelter ruins alongside the more modern Texaco abandonment.

The smelter overlooked the town and was once covered in smokestacks and buildings.

The land scarred by mining shows signs of regrowth among the ruins.

The peak behind the smelter has a 450-foot vertical tunnel, which was dug to try and rid the town of the overhanging smoke produced by the smelter.

Above: The Clifton power station.

Opposite page: An abandoned Texaco maintenance shed.

TEXACO

Above: The remains of the historical society museum.

Right: The museum doors have crosses carved into them, reminiscent of a church.

Opposite page: The crumbling interior of the museum.

A window frame inside the old adobe museum.

Brightly colored walls and fireplace are now scarred with peeling paint.

A fire damaged rear room of the museum with a crippled door frame.

A wall exposing the original adobe brick of the museum, which was reportedly built in the 1880s.

A former miner's home bulit into the hillside overlooking Clifton.

A more modern-day abandoned structure which was built after the 1983 flood.

The weathered facade of a home overlooking the San Francisco River.

A former miner's home with a precariously balanced porch hangs onto the side of the hill.

Perched high atop a hill in Clifton, this home is succumbing to nature.

One of Clifton's more modern homes showing signs of neglect.

The kitchen of the abandoned home with appliances still in place.

Above: Clifton's main street where striking miners marched in 1915–1916.

Opposite page: The arched facade is all that remains of the Lyric theatre.

Previous page: A weather-damaged, up-turned chair in the home's former living room.

An exposed wall of the Cascarelli building adjacent to the Lyric theatre.

The former Antonio Spezia's Hay & Grain Store.

The Clifton Social Club sign hanging by a thread.

A poem stapled to a fence post, describing the good old days of the 96 Ranch, greets visitors.

THE 96 RANCH

Tucked away in Pinal County's Ninetysix Hills area, between Florence and Dudleyville, the 'Ole 96 Ranch welcomes visitors with a lively poem reflecting upon the bygone era of cowboys and adventure. Recorded history, our factual narrative of the past, oftentimes fails to elicit the emotional response faded memories produce and lacks the vivid aliveness of shared stories. There is little to no historical information available about the 96 Ranch and, sadly, once the descendants of the original landowners pass, the stories will also, like the ranch, disintegrate into time.

Sometime around 1919–1920, the ranch was owned by Columbus Reed (Tump) Freeman. His grandson, Henry, remembers, clearly, the neighboring Three C Ranch, which his family also owned and where he grew up, but his memories of the 96 are hazy at best. When the ranch ceased operating is anyone's guess; the deteriorating adobe ranch home, outer buildings, and large barn offer up only eerie silence or the spine-tingling reverberation of a disturbed rattlesnake in response. The 88 square miles of Sonoran Desert the 96 Ranch encompasses is currently owned by a Canadian company.

Towering, sentry-like saguaros line the approach to the ranch. Their alignment, height, and circumference suggest they were planted deliberately. They have stood majestically throughout the decades, watching the comings and goings of the area's wildlife and the ranch's workers. They will guard the 96 Ranch until its final days and keep its secrets until they too succumb to the inevitable.

The 96 Ranch's adobe ranch house.

The 96 Ranch, surrounded by pristine sonoran desert.

The wood paneled back porch of the ranch house.

The view from the former living room.

The 96's large barn still stands, but its wooden exterior shows signs of deterioration.

Looking through a stock-holding area to a farmworker's former home.

The exterior of a weathered shed on the 96's land.

The almost-roofless interior of the shed.

Above: One of the many outer buildings in a state of decay.

Previous page: The stairway down to the underground meat cellar/cold room.

A disused tire basks in the afternoon sunlight.

An outer building without a roof or window.

Above: A ranch worker's decaying house, long ago disconnected from the dangling power lines.

Opposite page: A windmill with only a few remaining blades sits adjacent to the stockyard.

COTTON GIN

Searing heat rises visibly through the dust along the stretch of State Route 287 between Casa Grande and Coolidge. The vista of brown unsown farmland, broken only by the shocking green of cotton plants bears witness to almost a century of cotton farming in Pinal County. The history of modern-day cotton farming in Arizona began as early the 1880s and was spearheaded by blacksmith F. G. Hardwicke and A. J. Chandler, founder of the City of Chandler, who in 1899 successfully grew 5 acres of cotton. From this humble beginning, cotton grew to become one of Arizona's five "C's": Copper, Cattle, Cotton, Citrus, and Climate.

As the cotton industry boomed, so too did the need for cotton gins. Patented by U.S. inventor Eli Whitney in 1794, the cotton gin ("gin" derived from the word "engine") effectively and efficiently removed the seeds from cotton plants. The gin automated this once-tedious task and, as with the invention of the printing press, historians credit it with altering human history and shepherding in the industrial revolution.

At the intersection of 11-Mile Corner and State Route 287, gins dominate two corners. While one is still an active business surrounded by cotton farms, the other sits desolate and decaying, its corrugated steel clanging with the desert winds. It has become a lonely symbol of an industry in decline and the fate of its counterpart will be determined in the years ahead as farming practices evolve with the county's ever-changing economy.

The seed auger, where the seed fell and was sorted into separate piles.

Looking through the gin to the rear entrance and the parched desert.

A line of feeders exposed to the elements by the failing roof.

The feeder and many of its no longer operational parts.

A blaster wheel covered in thick cobwebs.

Above: The exterior of the gin. The white funnel is called the trash cyclone.

Opposite page: Two double-stack feeders.

The Lummus feeder.

Cotton left behind in the feeder from when the gin was active.

Gin stand levers.

A thick layer of dust covers the rusting feeder.

Detail of the gin stand where the seed is separated from the cotton.

Levers on the gin stand used to adjust for the variety of cotton being processed.

Pulley wheels on the feeders.

A broken window inside the gin.

Above: The view from the office of the gin through a broken window with dangling Venetian blinds.

Opposite page: The windowless former office deteriorates in the scorching desert heat.

A large circular incinerator burned the cotton waste before trailers were in use.

Gears and chains on the side of the feeder.

The feeder mechanism creates an interesting geometric pattern.

An aerial view of the Copper Hill Mill foundation.

COPPER HILL MINE

Stark concrete artifacts, crumbling and adorned with obligatory graffiti, rise awkwardly from the desert landscape, announcing the presence of what was once the mining settlement of Copper Hill. Underground tunnels reminiscent of bomb shelters are burrowed deep into the hillside and are guarded by large beehives. Most of what remains of Copper Hill is located on private land and it is hard to imagine a community of 500 once inhabited what is now picturesque ranching land.

Copper Hill existed as a mining camp owned, prior to 1905, by the Copper Hill group. The mine ceased operations in 1910 after the financial failure of its president but was soon operational again under the reorganized Arizona Commercial Mining Company. Between 1906 and 1930, the mine produced 92,000,000 pounds of copper. Interestingly, for a town with such a short lifespan, little more than thirty years between the early 1900s and the late 1930s, it offered more than the usual stores, boarding houses, and offices; it was also the site of a hospital and school. Copper Hill's post office was established in 1908 and closed in 1933, and, reportedly, five years later only forty residents remained.

Enclosed on three sides by the dramatically beautiful Tonto National Forest, the land that was once Copper Hill seems, outwardly at least, recovered from the brutality of mining. Cows roam lazily along Copper Hill Road, and the few residents who now call the area home are disturbed only by the occasional off-road enthusiast and interested explorers searching for another piece of Arizona's mining history.

Surrounded by the Tonto National Forest, the Copper Hill Mining District boasts stunning views.

Rays of the setting sun highlight the graffiti-covered ruins.

The entranceway to one of the underground tunnels.

Partial equipment remains.

The foundations with rebar protruding through the concrete

A concrete tunnel-like structure above the mill foundation.

Storm clouds building over the mill's ruins.

From every angle, the mill ruins offer views of Tonto National Forest.

Many of the Copper Hill District ruins sit on privately owned land, yet this does not seem to deter graffiti artists.

Foundations can be found along a mile-long stretch of Copper Hill Road.

Foundation pillars frame the desert landscape.

Crumbling walls surrounded by concrete rubble.

A disused headframe.

The decaying headframe looks to be sliding down the hillside.

Rotting wood spans the headframe above the mine shaft.

A rusted-out car and mining equipment in front of what remains of the original schoolhouse.

Disused mining equipment litters the land.

The original post office and general store is now part of a ranch and used for storage.

Above and Opposite: Pillars that once supported the mining structures.

Archways within the concrete block support.

COOLIDGE/CASA GRANDE FARMS

Dinosaurs of central Arizona's early agricultural period litter the barren landscape of Pinal County's forgotten farms. Replaced by the behemoth Terminator-like machinery of our modern era, wooden-spoked wheels, and tractors with rusted-out seats lay idle where they once worked the land of small family-owned farms. Today, much of the land is owned by multi-national conglomerates and leased back to farmers. While some of the larger family-owned and operated farms are still in existence, they are among the ever-dwindling minority.

Casa Grande and Coolidge's prosperity mirrored that of the country's. In 1920, there were almost 300 farms covering more than 150,000 acres in Pinal County. During the next decade, the number of farms in the area tripled and the amount of farmed acreage doubled. The prosperity was short lived though, as the Depression hit and land prices plummeted. The takeover of the small and mid-sized family-owned farms began in 1935. Large industrial farmers consumed their smaller counterparts as they were better able to absorb the losses brought about by the Depression and lack of irrigation.

Today, wandering through the antiquated farming equipment and the desolate remains of farmhouses, it is hard not to wonder what comes next for the area. Will the remaining prosperous farms withstand rising irrigation costs and further water shortages? Or will the rapidly encroaching urban sprawl swallow these remaining farms and their proud lineage?

Arid farmland surrounds a long abandoned farmhouse.

Disused farming equipment rots in the searing desert heat.

An outer building on the farm property.

A corroded roto mulcher sits idle.

A vintage tractor shielded from the weather by a primitive shelter.

An old steel-belted tire, cracked from the heat.

Above: The tractor's tires are sinking into the dry earth.

Opposite page: A steering wheel frozen in time.

A vintage seed spreader.

A rusting tiller sinks into the ground.

A tumbleweed trapped in a concrete holding area.

A decrepit drum sits among other disused equipment.

A small, disused milking shed adjacent to active farmland.

The view from the farmhouse is barren and desolate.

Stripped of much of its exterior, this former farmworker's home is destined to collapse.

Sunlight and shadows inside a small home.

Heavy cobwebs span the kitchen sink area.

Kitchen cupboards flung open by curious visitors.

Tall grass surrounds the buildings on the property.

The sheet metal roof is lifting away from the frame.

An old wooden crate bathed in the late afternoon sun is covered in cobwebs and dirt.

Farming machinery from a bygone era.

Stripped tires surround rusty rims on equipment that no longer has a use.

A flat tire, in the true sense of the word, on a wooden spoked wheel.

Crates, imprinted with the farm name, are stacked to the ceiling in a large shed.

A maintenance shed with its contents strewn throughout the abandoned space.

An area of wall has collapsed from neglect.

A beehive-like charcoal kiln, referred to by locals as a "coke oven."

FLORENCE CHARCOAL KILNS

Secrets and oddities abound in Arizona's desert wilderness and few are as difficult to access as the spectacularly strange and colloquially named "coke ovens." Rising like giant beehives from the desert floor, the more than 125-year-old "ovens" are in fact charcoal kilns. According to historians, they were used to make mesquite charcoal for smelting ores at nearby mines. Located across the Gila River from the now-vanished town of Cochran, their inaccessibility has ensured they remain largely untouched.

Construction of the huge stone kilns from granite and dacite was completed sometime in the latter part of the 1800s, and they loom over the surrounding desert at a height of 26 feet. Little factual information is available, which adds fuel to the tall tales that have graced the pages of newspapers and spurned conversations around campfires. One such elaborate theory, proposed by an old prospector in the 1970s, suggests they were lead smelters built by the Phoenicians who came to the area in 1500 to convert the Native Americans and whom he credits with founding the city of Phoenix.

Another entertaining tale claims they were built a thousand years ago by Montezuma, who was assisted by various Mormon angels. These tales are as fantastical as the journey to the infamous "coke ovens," and while history shows us there is no truth in them, there are some certainties surrounding these oddities that do exist; the trek to the charcoal kilns will continue to be rugged and claim many vehicle axles and leave many ardent explorers stranded, where they may very well encounter an old-time prospector with his own theory of how the "coke ovens" came to be.

An entry to a long disused kiln.

The interior of a charcoal kiln.

Above: The row of kilns looking east.

Opposite page: A tenacious cactus pushes its way through the stone exterior.

Cloudy skies looming over the kilns.

It is not surprising the kilns are said to resemble beehives, they create an odd sight in the desert.

Sunlight breaks through the clouds and streams into a kiln.

EDEN

Arizona ghost towns typically regale visitors and researchers with tales of outlaws, shoot-outs, scoundrels, and intrepid adventurers seeking their fortune—Eden breaks the mold. Founded in 1881 by Mormon settlers, Moses Curtis and William Hawkins, the town was initially called Curtis. The opening of the post office in 1882 saw the name changed to Eden for the Garden of Eden in the Hebrew Bible. The town's main street, crisscrossed with ironically named streets such as Merry Land Lane and Wonder Lane, lays interrupted by sweeping views of agricultural properties and lined with abandoned stores and homes.

Naturally graced with hot springs, the area just north of Eden's town center, became the site of the Indian Hot Springs Hotel. The noble three-story Victorian-style building, described by historian William Ryder Ridgeway as a "feudal castle," accumulated more than a century of colorful history before burning to the ground in 2008. Hundreds of years before the commercialization of the springs, Native Americans and Spanish explorers utilized the healing properties of Eden's natural springs to soothe their weariness.

Despite its inauspicious start as a farming community, Eden boasts several claims to fame, among them: visits by rock superstar Mick Jagger; as the set location for the horror film *The Gay Bed and Breakfast of Terror;* the 1970s and 1980s saw it become a popular nudist colony; and, more ominously, a murder-suicide took place there in 2002. Today, it is hard to imagine this semi-ghost town has any roles left to play as its remaining structures slowly vanish back into the surrounding desert.

EDEN STORE

Above: The rear of Eden's general store. *Previous page:* The desolate Eden Store.

The roof and walls of the store are collapsing.

Looking out from inside the Eden store, across the lightly traveled road, to the general merchandise.

The shell of the general merchandise is supported by large wooden props.

Eden's abandoned church.

The crumbling stage of the church.

The church is mostly roofless, and as the walls collapse, it is hard to imagine it will remain standing much longer.

Eden's post office, covered by overgrown weeds.

A once-expensive couch inside the post office.

The deserted home of a former Eden resident.

A garden shed behind the abandoned home.

The Eden Schoolhouse is, like most of the other buildings in the town, decaying in the brutal desert climate.

What remains of the interior of the school.

A discarded shopping cart and other junk litters the school property.

A discarded teddy bear tells its own tale of neglect.

BIBLIOGRAPHY

"96 Ranch Pinal County" Retrieved July 1, 2019 from www.headquarterswest.com/listings/96/

"Arizona Commercial Mine, Old Dominion vein system, Black Peak area, Copper Hill, Globe Hills, Globe Hills District, Globe-Miami District, Gila Co., Arizona, USA" Retrieved July 20, 2019 from www.mindat.org/loc-61634.html

Becker, S. A., Murder, Suicide Hit Eden Hot Springs. *Eastern Arizona Courier*. February 27, 2002 Retrieved July 16, 2019 from www.eacourier.com/news/murder-suicide-hit-eden-hot-springs/article_092f4c69-3099-5a72-9012-5db88998ef0b.html

Borade, G., "Step Back in Time - How Does the Cotton Gin Actually Work?." Historyplext, March 19, 2018. Retrieved August 6, 2019 from, historyplex.com/how-does-cotton-gin-work

Ives, R. L., "The Cochran Coke Ovens." *The Journal of Arizona History, vol. 13, no. 2*, 1972, pp. 73–81

Keane, M., "COTTON AND FIGS: The Great Depression in the Casa Grande Valley." *The Journal of Arizona History, vol. 32, no. 3*, 1991, pp. 267–290. Retrieved July 28, 2019 JSTOR, www.jstor.org/stable/41695889.

Lucas, R., "Indian Hot Springs Was Really Hot" Arizona100 Blogspot, April 11, 2010. Retrieved July 16, 2019 from arizona100.blogspot.com/2010/04/indian-hot-springs-was-really-hot-among.html

"Mining Ruins, Globe, Arizona" Retrieved July 20, 2019 from www.ghosttownaz.info/copper-hill-mill-site.php

Sowders, S. D., "A ship lost in the desert: The Indian Hot Springs Hotel, Part 1." *Eastern Arizona Courier*. November 18, 2015, Retrieved July 16, 2019 from www.eacourier.com/lifestyle/a-ship-lost-in-the-desert-the-indian-hot-springs/article_7d5740d2-8d5d-11e5-ab4d-33b6fb8fd143.html

Sowders, S. D., "One of the finest: The Indian Hot Springs Hotel, Part 2." *Eastern Arizona Courier*. November 21, 2015, Retrieved July 16, 2019 from www.eacourier.com/lifestyle/one-of-the-finest-the-indian-hot-springs-hotel-part/article_cb993268-8fde-11e5-8cf5-43fdbf223d2a.html

Sowders, S. D., "Postcards and rock stars: The Indian Hot Springs Hotel, Part 3." *Eastern Arizona Courier*. November 25, 2015, Retrieved July 16, 2019 from www.eacourier.com/lifestyle/postcards-and-rock-stars-the-indian-hot-springs-hotel-part/article_f66e9884-9308-11e5-be5e-4bb7d390d1cb.html

Villarreal, P., "Gay Horror Flick Screens at the Loft." Tuscon.com, March 15, 2008. Retrieved July 16, 2019 from tucson.com/entertainment/gay-horror-flick-screens-at-the-loft/article_a7d15bd5-8bda-52f7-b91c-1fb6dd5025ca.html

Vinson, M. C., "VANISHED CLIFTON-MORENCI: An Architect's Perspective." *The Journal of Arizona History, vol. 33, no. 2*, 1992, pp. 183–206. Retrieved from July 28, 2019 from JSTOR, www.jstor.org/stable/41695935.

Walking Tour of Historic Chase Creek Street: Clifton Arizona, www.cometoclifton.com/sights-to-see/walking-tour.php, Come to Clifton, Retrieved July 28

Weiser-Alexander, K., "Eden, Arizona – Mormon Ghost Town" Legends of America, May, 2019. Retrieved July 16, 2019 from www.legendsofamerica.com/eden-arizona/